iPAD AIR: USER GUIDE

Step By Step Guide To Understand key Features With Your iPad Air For Beginners Seniors and professionals

By

Robert A Bernard

Copyright © 2020 Robert A Bernard

All rights reserved. No part of this book shall be reproduced, stored in a retrieval system, or transmitted by any means, electronic, mechanical, photocopying, recording, or otherwise, without written permission from the publisher. Although every precaution has been taken in the preparation of this book, the publisher and author assume no responsibility for errors or omissions. Nor is any liability assumed for damages resulting from the use of the information contained herein.

Table of Contents

CHAPTER ONE 1

APPLE IPAD AIR 2020: THE REVIEW 1

CHAPTER TWO 6

iPAD AIR SET UP 6

CHAPTER THREE 12

PRIVACY AND SECURITY ... 12

CHAPTER FOUR.................. 20

SIRI.. 20

CHAPTER FIVE 27

iPAD AIR TOUCH ID........... 27

CHAPTER SIX 33

SAFARI 33

CHAPTER SEVEN 41

APPLE PAY 41

CHAPTER EIGHT 51

BOOKS 51

CHAPTER NINE	60
iTunes STORE	60
CHAPTER TEN	69
MUSIC	69
CHAPTER ELEVEN	77
APPS	77
CHAPTER TWELVE	85
MAPS	85
CHAPTER THIRTEEN	95
KEYBOARD	95
CHAPTER FOURTEEN	102
REMINDER	102
CHAPTER FIFTEEN	111
HOME APP	111

NEW iPAD AIR
2020

iPAD AIR

CHAPTER ONE

APPLE IPAD AIR 2020: THE REVIEW

If you want to get an iPad now you can afford it, it's the best tablet for most people. Apple took the design from the more expensive Pro and brought it to the right price. but this year's iPad Air upgrade has a bigger, better screen and a faster and more interesting processor.

It's also one of the most enjoyable computing experiences you'll ever experience. iPad may not have the full flexibility of desktop operating systems like Windows or macOS, but it is much easier to use.

iPad Air Design

The new iPad Air 2020 is moving to the double-sided version of the case and the round screen we first saw in 2018 on the iPad Pro. Back then, Nail Patel said the design "looked a little ugly - almost the same as the driver's design." I've gotten used to it in the intervening years, and it's clearly the same at Apple.

At the back is a wide-angle 12-megapixel camera

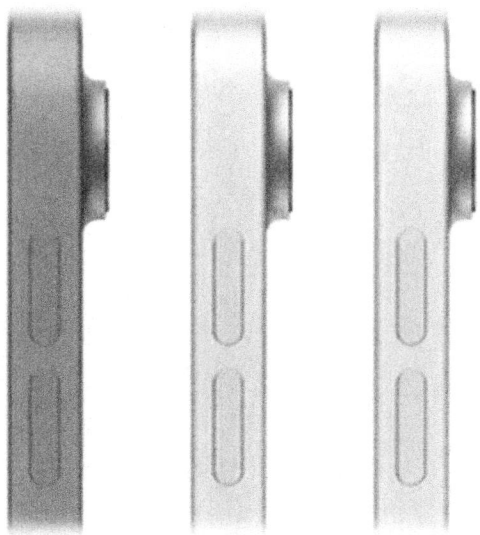

The hardware work on the tablet disappears and goes well here. If you want another brand, Apple is offering new colors for the aluminum frame. In addition to the usual silver, gray, and rose gold, it is now green and light blue.

The Air iPad switches from electric to USB-C charging, such as the Pro. I applaud this wholeheartedly - USB-C is a great addition to the port and unlocks the iPad for many things, including other similar things you can use on your laptop

However, if you are replacing an older iPad, note that the cable is different. Note that this new design means that iPad uses Air Pro mode devices.

The last point of the design: the front camera is on the side when you hold the iPad in a horizontal position.

Then adjust your eyes to look right or left when you call Zoom. Or set the camera to completely off because iPadOS will turn off immediately when you start any multitasking.

Apart from the new colors, there is only an external difference between the Pro and the air, both of which are subtle. The iPad Air screen is technically smaller, 10.9 inches diagonally instead of 11 of other devices.

CHAPTER TWO

iPAD AIR SET UP

Turn on and set up the iPad

Activate and set up your new iPad online. You can configure it by connecting the iPad to your computer. You can also transfer your data and files to your new iPad. if you have a device such as an iPhone, iPad, iPod touch, or Android device

Prepare for setup

To make the set as smooth as possible, you must have the following:

Internet connection over a Wi-Fi network (network name and password may be required) or mobile data service (Wi-Fi + mobile models)

Apple ID and password; If you don't have an Apple ID, you can do so during setup

Activate and set up your iPad

Hold down the up button until the Apple logo appears.

Looking at the back of the top of the iPad, the phone shows the top button in the upper left corner.

If the iPad isn't activated, you may need to charge the battery

Do one of the following:

Tap the setting manually, and then follow the on-screen configuration instructions.

If you're using iOS 11, iPadOS 13, or any other iPhone, iPad, or iPod touch, you can use Quick Start to set up your new device automatically. You can pair devices and follow the onscreen instructions to securely copy settings, preferences, and most of your iCloud keychain. You can then restore all the data and content in the iCloud repository to your new device.

If your devices are running iOS 12.4, iPadOS 13, or later, you can transfer all data from your previous device to your device without a phone. Keep the device

ON until the transition process is complete.

If you are blind or visually impaired, press the Home button three times (on the iPad with the home button) or the button three times (on some iPad models) to open the screen reader audio. You can double-tap the screen with three fingers to unlock the zoom.

Move from Android device to iPad

When you first set up your first iPad, you can automatically move and save data on an Android device.

Note: You can only use motion in the iOS app once you start setting up the iPad app. To complete the installation and use navigation for iOS, you must deactivate and restart the iPad or manually move your data.

Set up mobile service on iPad (Wi-Fi + and mobile models)

If you have a Wi-Fi + mobile model, you can sign up for a mobile data plan. This allows you to connect to the Internet via a Wi-Fi network.

You can set up a mobile data plan for any of the following:

eSIM

Set up your mobile package via eSIM

For models that support ESIM, you can enable mobile service on your iPad. You can send your iPad abroad and register for a mobile service with your local manager. This option is not available in all countries or regions and does not support all supported content.

Select Settings> Mobile Data.

Do one of the following:

To set up the first cell phone set up on the iPad, select a keypad, and follow the onscreen instructions.

To add another mobile device to your iPad, tap Install New Setting.

CHAPTER THREE

PRIVACY AND SECURITY

Set the password to iPad

For added security, set the password you need to enter to unlock the iPad when you turn it on or off. Setting a password also unlocks data protection, encrypting iPad data with 256-bit AES encryption. (Some applications may choose to opt-out of data security.)

Edit or change the code

Go to Settings, depending on the type, click one of the following:

- Face ID and encoding code

- Touch the ID and password

- Standard code

Tap Unlock Password or Change Password.

To view the Reset Password option, select Password Settings. Security options are the standard alphanumeric code and the standard numeric code.

To view the Reset Password option, select Password Settings. Security options are the standard alphanumeric code and the standard numeric code.

Once you've set the password, you can use Face ID or Touch ID to unlock the iPad for supported modes. However, for added security, you must enter your password to unlock the iPad under the following conditions:

You can activate or restart the iPad.

You have not unlocked your iPad for more than 48 hours.

He unlocked his iPad with a code 6.5 days ago and hasn't unlocked it with Face ID or Touch ID in the last 4 hours.

IPad will receive a remote lock command.

Toggle when iPad locks automatically

Select Settings> Display & light> Auto lock and set the time limit.

Delete data after 10 failed codes

You can set to erase all information, media, and personal settings after ten consecutive attempts to decode the iPad.

Go to Settings, depending on the type, click one of the following:

• Face ID and encoding code

• Touch the ID and password

• Standard code

• Enable data deletion.

After deleting all data, you must restore or restore the iPad backup.

Delete the password

Go to Settings, depending on the type, click one of the following:

• Face ID and encoding code

- Touch the ID and password

- Standard code

- Touch to delete the password.

- Code reset

If you enter an incorrect password six times at a time, you will receive a message that your device is locked and your iPad is locked. If you can't remember your password, you can delete it in iPad Electronic or recovery mode and then set a new password. (If you made an iCloud or computer copy before you forgot your password, you can restore the data and settings in the archive.)

Contact Apple Support if you forgot your password on your iPad.

Set the Face ID on iPad

Using Face ID (supported forms), you can securely and easily unlock iPad, authorize purchases and payments, and access many third-party programs on your iPad.

To use Face ID, you need to set a password on the iPad.

Set the Face ID or add another look

To set Touch ID, go to Settings> Face ID and Password> Face ID and follow the on-screen instructions.

To set up another profile face, tap Settings> Face ID and password> Set another view, and follow the instructions on the screen.

Face ID activation screen. The face appears on the screen, enclosed in a circle. The text below instructs you to move your head slightly to fill the circle.

If you have a physical barrier, click Accessibility when setting your face ID. Once this is done, face recognition is not required for a complete list of head movements. Face ID is safe to use, but you need to keep an eye on your iPad.

Face ID also has an access point that you can use for the blind or visually impaired. If you don't need a face ID, you need to look at the iPad with your eyes open, go to Settings> Accessibility> Face ID and Care, and listen to Face ID. This article automatically shuts off when you enable audio reception when you start setting up the iPad. See Changing Face ID and Configuration Settings on the iPad.

Temporarily disable the face ID

You can temporarily disable Face ID when you unlock your iPad.

Press and hold the volume key and another volume key for 2 seconds.

CHAPTER FOUR

SIRI

Ask Siri on the iPad

Talking to Siri is the fastest way to do things. Ask Siri to translate the sentence, set the time, find a place, report the weather, and much more. The more you use Siri, the better you know what you need.

To use Siri, connect your iPad to the Internet. Mobile payments can work.

Use the button on the bottom of the iPad to continue the conversation with Siri.

Adjust the Siri

On the iPad, click Settings> Siri & Search, and then do the following:

If you want to call Siri with your voice: say, "Hey Siri."

Call Siri with the key: Open Siri with the home key or you can press the top key of Siri.

To change additional Siri settings, see Change iPad Siri settings.

Call Siri With Voice

When you call Siri with your voice, Siri answers aloud.

Ask Siri a question or get a job if you say, "Hey Siri."

To ask another question to Siri or perform another task, say the word "Hey Siri" again or click the Attention button.

Note: To prevent the iPad from responding to the "Hey Siri" message, drop your iPad, or go to Settings> Siri and Search and listen to "Hey Siri".

You can say "Hey Siri" to Siri while wearing an AirPods Pro or Airpods (2nd generation). Try using Siri with AirPods on your iPad.

Call Siri with the key

Siri responds silently when you dial with the Siri button and mute the iPad. To change this, try changing Siri's response.

Do one of the following:

22

On the iPad with the Home button: Press the Home button.

For other iPad models: Press the up button.

Remote EarPods and microphone: (sold separately) Press and hold the hub or call button.

When Siri appears, ask Siri a question or type the question yourself.

Call Siri by pressing or holding Airpods, or double-clicking. Try using Siri with AirPods on your iPad.

If Siri doesn't understand you well, make repairs

Repeat your request: Press the Listen button, then say something else.

Part of the request by Spelling: Click Attention, then repeat your request by typing words you don't understand. For example, enter the person's name by saying "call."

Change it before sending the message: Say the word "Change".

Edit your request with the text: If you see your request on the screen, you can edit it. Click the application and then use the on-screen keyboard.

Type instead of talking to Siri

Select Settings> Accessibility> Siri and enable the Siri type.

To apply, call Siri and then use the keyboard and text area to ask Siri a question or get a job done.

If Siri doesn't work as expected on your iPad, see the Apple Support article for Siri.

Siri is designed to protect your information and you can choose what you share with others

What Siri can do on your iPad

Use Siri on the iPad for information and functionality. Siri's response is more visible than what it does, allowing her to focus on the information that appears on the screen.

Siri is working together. When Siri displays a web link, you can click it to see more details in the browser. If you add buttons or controls to the screen response from Siri, you can press them to activate. Click again to ask another question or do extra work.

Finding answers to questions: searching for information on the Internet, searching for sports articles, math, and more Say: Hey sir, what is the reason for the rain?

CHAPTER FIVE

iPAD AIR TOUCH ID

The iPad Air is the first Apple device to feature or have a fingerprint reader that is located under the power button.

The fourth version of the iPad Air offers a completely new design, just like the Pad Pro. The fresh air has a flat edge, the home button drains and adds USB-C ports. Apple used the same design and configuration as the iPhone 12, retaining the USB-C port. But one thing I don't care about is Apple's face recognition, face ID. Instead, you will open your tablet with your finger, agreeing to purchase and access apps.

On a mobile device, we first see a new identification sensor that is hidden under the power button. Or, as Apple calls it, "the top button." When the iPad holds air vertically, you'll find a button in the upper right corner, near the corner. When paired with features like the Apple Magic keyboard, it will be on the left, near the top.

Apple is not the first company to use these types of fingerprint sensors. The Microsoft Surface Duo and most Samsung Galaxy phones have the same biometric settings.

set-up-touch-id-ipad-air

During the initial setup, log in and register your fingerprint with Touch ID.

The installation process will be the same. although the sensor is now on the iPad Air.

During the initial setup, you will be asked to place your finger on the user several times, lift and adjust each reading to teach you the Apple Secure Enclave

You can repeat this process up to five times, with different fingers each time, or sign up to re-read the same finger to provide more data for different categories.

If you have skipped the previous ID settings or want to enroll more than one finger, you can add them at any time by opening the Settings app and opening the ID and password. Then enter your PIN, click Fingerprint, and follow the steps.

Just leave your finger on the second divider button and it will magically open.

How to open, access apps, and buy items with Touch ID

The top button on the iPad Air works the same as the home button on previous generations of the iPad and iPhones.

You can press a button to wake up the iPad and turn it on at the same time, or if the iPad is already awake, you need to put your finger on the button until the device opens and goes to the Home screen.

To access the app or accept a purchase, simply place your finger on the button without pushing inward. It only takes a fraction of a second to analyze print to unlock iPad mobile devices, confirm

Apple-ipad-air-touch-id-security

Apple attaches a new Apple Air TOUCH ID to the button on the side of the iPad.

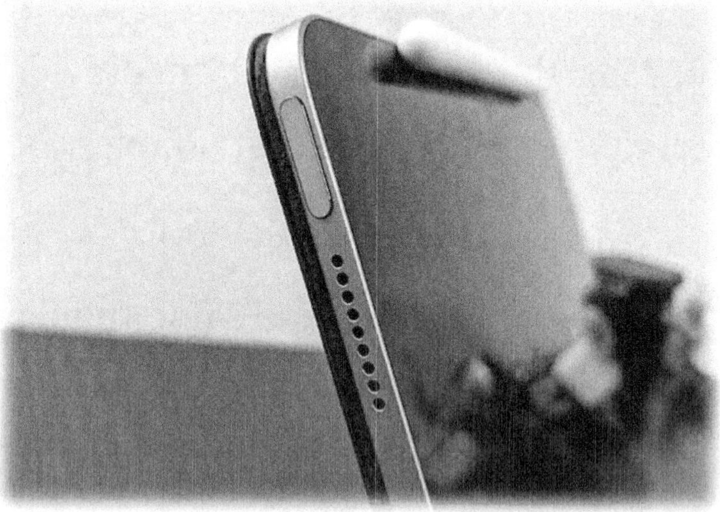

CHAPTER SIX

SAFARI

You can add a webpage, browse the web to your reading list for later reading, and also add page icons to your Home screen for your quick access.

If you sign in to iCloud with the same Apple ID and password on all your devices, you can also see your open pages on other devices and keep your bookmarks, history, and updated lists on all your devices.

Above this control, open the webpage in Safari from left to right: back, forward, and bookmark buttons, address space, assignment, new tabs, and page buttons.

You can easily browse a website with a few taps.

Back to top: Double-click the top of the screen to quickly return to the top of the long page.

See Top of Page: Moving iPad to the Area.

To refresh the page: Click the Reload button next to the title in the search box.

To share links: Click the Share button

Change text size, display, and site settings

IPad displays a version of the Safari desktop site that automatically scales to iPad display and optimizes color installation.

In the View menu, you can increase or decrease the text size, switch to page view, set privacy limits, and more.

To open the View menu, click the Select button on the website to the left of the search box, and then do the following:

To change the font size: Press the large key to increase the font size and the A key to decrease it.

To view a webpage without ads or navigation menus: Click to view reading (if any).

To hide the search area: Tap Hide Toolbar (Click at the top of the screen to download).

View the mobile version of the website: Click to request a website (if any).

To set the view and privacy controls **when you visit this site**: Click Site Settings.

See two pages on each side of the split view

Use Split View to open both sides of Safari.

To open a blank page in split view: Press and hold Page, and then click New Windows.

Open the link in split view: Press and hold the link, and then click Open in Windows.

To move a window to the other side of the view: Hold down the top of the window and drag it left or right.

To close tabs in partition windows: Click and hold the Page button.

To place the split view: Drag the area above the window you want to close.

Preview links to your site

Touch and hold the Safari link to view the online view without opening the page. Click on the view or select an option to open a link.

Click anywhere outside the show to close the show and stay on the current page.

Excellence by displaying the destination title and possible list: Open, open in a new tab, open from a shared view, add to a reading list, copy, or share.

Translate the website

Translate text on a website using Safari.

If you're viewing a webpage in another language, click Select a website, and then click Translate.

Copy management

Click the download button to view the size of the downloaded file, access the downloaded file immediately, or drag the downloaded file to another file or email you are working on.

You can download the files later when you continue to use Safari.

Use keyboard shortcuts

You can browse Safari using external keyboard shortcuts.

To view keyboard shortcuts, press and hold the Command key

web browsing

Enter a search term, phrase, or URL in the search section at the top of the page.

Click on the navigation bar to find exactly what you typed or go to the keyboard.

At the top of the screen is the Safari search bar labeled "Cupertino Weather." Below the search area, the current weather and the temperature of Cupertino are displayed. Below are Google search results, including

"Cabinet Weather," "Clock Cabinet Weather," "Yesterday's Cabinet Weather," and "Year-Round Cabinet Weather." The blue arrow to the right of each hit points to the results page

CHAPTER SEVEN

APPLE PAY

Set up Apple Pay for apps in iPad Air

With Apple Pay, you can make secure payments in apps and websites that support Apple Pay. Messaging lets you send and receive money from friends and family, and make purchases with business chats.

Add a credit or debit card

Choose Settings> Wallet and Apple Payments.

Tap to add cards. sign in using your Apple ID.

Do one of the following:

Add a new card: Insert iPad as shown on the card, or enter the card information manually.

Add your previous cards: choose the Apple ID, and Apple Payments on other devices, or the cards that you have removed. Click Continue, and then enter the CVV number for each card.

Alternatively, you can add your card to a banking application or debit card.

The card issuer will determine if your card is eligible for Apple Payment, and you can request additional information to complete the verification process.

View card information and change settings

Choose Settings> Wallet and Apple Payments.

Tap the card, then do one of the following:

To view the latest history, tap Transactions. Clear your transaction history to hide this information. See your card issuer's report to see all Apple Payments activity.

See the number of the last four cards and the account number of the device - the number forwarded to the merchant.

Change the account address.

Remove the card from the Apple Pay app.

Change Apple Pay settings

Choose Settings> Wallet and Apple Payments.

Do the following:

Set the default card.

Enter shipping addresses and purchase contact information.

If your iPad is lost or stolen, remove your card from the Apple Pay app

If you have access to My iPhone, you can use it to locate and protect your iPad.

To remove your card from Apple Pay, follow these steps:

On a Mac or PC: Sign in with your Apple ID. In the Tools section, click Lost iPad. Click Delete All at the end of the card list.

On another iPhone, iPad, or iPod touch: Go to Settings> [Your Name], click the lost iPad, and then click Delete All Cards (under Apple Pay).

Input your cards.

If you remove the cards, you can reassemble them later.

If you turn off iCloud Settings> [your name], all Apple Pay credit and debit cards will be removed from the iPad. You can pick up the cards again the next time you log in.

Note: Apple's payment capabilities and features vary by country and region.

Use the Apple Pay app for iPad apps, app photos, and Safari

You can shop with Safari wherever you see apps, app clips, and the Apple Pay button on the web.

An application that shows the product page with the Buy Payment with the Apple Payment button.

Pay for an app, app clip, or web

Click the Apple Pay button when you exit.

Overview of payment information.

You can change your credit card, shipping address, and contact information.

Full payment:

For iPad with Touch ID: Confirm with an ID or press your code.

For an iPad with a Face ID: Double-click the button above, then access the iPad to authenticate with the ID or enter your password.

Change the default presentation and communication information

Choose Settings> Wallet and Apple Payments.

- Delivery Address

- E-mail

• Phones

Find and use Apple money on iPad (the U.S. only)

When you receive money from messages, add them to Apple's money. You can use Apple Cash immediately, wherever you use Apple Pay. You will also be able to transfer Apple's cash balance to your bank account.

The details in the upper right corner of the Apple Cash Card screen show the balance.

Schedule Apple Cash

Do the following:

Go to Settings> Wallet and Apple Payments, then open Apple Money.

Send or receive payment in messages. View payments in apps or on the web using Apple Pay.

Use Apple Money

• Use Apple Pay to use Apple Money anywhere:

• You can receive money through Apple Pay

• Send money via Apple Pay

• Pay for applications or from the Internet using Apple Pay

Manage Apple money

Go to Settings> Wallet and Apple Payments and click Apple Money.

Do the following:

- Add money to the debit card.
- Update your bank account information.

Tap Transactions to view history and details (e.g.

CHAPTER EIGHT

BOOKS

Find and buy audiobooks and audiobooks from the Apple Books app on iPad

In Books, you can find up-to-date merchants, browse the top lists, or select a list selected by Apple Book Editors. Once you have selected a book or audiobook, you can read or listen to the app once.

Open books to search for topics, click a bookstore or audiobook or click the Search button to view a specific topic or author.

Click on the book cover to see more information, read a sample, listen to a preview, or comment on what you want to read.

To buy the title, tap Buy, or click Download to download the free theme.

All purchases are made using the payment method associated with your Apple ID.

For iPad models connected to a mobile network, books and audiobooks can be automatically downloaded to the mobile network if you're not already connected to a Wi-Fi network. Choose Settings> Books, scroll to Mobile Data, select an instance, and click Enable.

Read books in the iPad book app

Read now: Tap to access the books and audiobooks you've read. Scroll down to view the books and audiobooks and sample books added to the study collection. You can set daily reading goals and take notes on books completed throughout the year.

Library: Tap to view all the books, audiobooks, series, and PDFs you find in a bookstore, or you can manually add them to your library. Click on the collection to read, categorize my samples, audiobooks, and books by completed categories.

Book system screen. At the bottom of the screen, from left to right, Read Now, Library, Bookstore, Audiobooks, and Search Tabs - the Reading tab is selected. At the top of the screen is the section you just read, which shows the current textbook. Below is a reading section listing the books you want to read.

Read a book

Click the current reading area or directory, and then click the cover to open the book. Use gestures and controls to move in the following direction:

Scroll: Click on the right side of the page or drag from left to right.

To go back to the previous page: left-click on the page or drag from left to right.

To navigate to a specific page: Click the page and slide the slide to the lower left or lower right corner of the screen. Alternatively, enter the page number by pressing the search button and then clicking the page number in the search results.

To close the book: Click the center of the page to display the controls, then click Back.

An open page of the booking system appears at the top of the screen, from left to right, showing the book's closure, table of contents, menu, visibility, and bookmarks.

Tip: Set iPad to landscape if you want to view two pages at once.

Once you've completed a book, personalized suggestions will help you find your next reading.

Modify text and display visibility

Click the page, click View, and then do one of the following:

Adjust screen brightness: Move the slider left or right of the device.

To change the font size: Press the large key to increase the font size and the A key to decrease it.

Change font: Press Font to select other fonts.

To change the color of the back of the page: Click the color wheel.

To dim the dark screen: Open the Auto Night theme to automatically change the color of the page and lighten it when you use books in bright conditions. (Not all books support spontaneous content at night.)

To disable the myth: Click Translate Text to scroll through the book or PDF.

From top to bottom, the visibility menu is selected to control brightness, font size, font, page color, automatic night theme, and navigation.

Bookmark

Press the bookmarks bar to add a bookmark; Click again to delete the bookmark.

To view all bookmarks, click Table of Contents, and then click Bookmarks.

Select or highlight text

Tap a word further, then remove the space

CHAPTER NINE

iTunes STORE

Use the iTunes Store to add music, movies, TV, and audio to your iPad

Note: The iTunes Store requires an Internet connection. The iTunes Store and its features vary by country or region.

Find music, movies, and TV shows

In the iTunes Store, call one of the following:

Music, movies, or TV: Browse by category To remove a search, click the categories at the top of the screen.

Top Spreadsheets: See iTunes Favorites.

Genius: Check out tips based on what you bought on iTunes.

Search: Type what you want, then click the Search button on your keyboard.

Click on an item to see more details. You can view songs, watch movie trailers and TV shows, or click the share button and do one of the following:

Share a link to the item: Select a sharing option.

Give something as a gift: Tap on the gift.

Add item to wishlist: Click to add to the wishlist.

To view the wish list, click the wish list, and then click the wish list.

Purchase and download content

Press the Value key to purchase an item. If the item is free, tap Download.

If you see the download button instead of the price, you've already purchased the item and can download it again for free.

If necessary, verify your Apple ID with a Face ID, Touch ID, or Password to complete your purchase.

To view the progress of the download, tap Download.

Get the sound sample

Click Music, click Categories, scroll down, and then click Sounds.

Browse by category or click on the charts above to see the most popular.

Click on the ringtone to see more details or play the scene.

To purchase a voice tag, press the Value key.

Use or submit the App Store and iTunes card

Tap the music and scroll down.

Use Gift or tap Send.

To find ringtones, alarm sounds and text ringtones, in the iTunes Store for iPad

In the iTunes Store, you can set ringtones, text tones, and other alarm clock alerts, and more. You can buy it.

Buy new sounds

In the iTunes Store, click Categories, and then click Sounds.

Click to find a specific song or artist by category or search.

Press a sound to view details or play a video.

To purchase sound, press the Value key.

Receive downloaded ringtones with your Apple ID

If you purchased the ringtones from another device, you can download them again.

Go to Settings> Sounds.

Click any sound below the sound and vibration patterns.

Touch to download all purchased ringtones. You may not recognize this option if you have already downloaded all purchased ringtones or have not yet purchased a ringtone.

You can manage iTunes Store purchases and settings on your iPad

In the iTunes Store, you or other family members can view and download purchased music, movies, and TV shows. You can customize the iTunes Store selection in Settings.

Purchase and family sharing agreement

Depending on the family agreement, the family helper can view and approve the purchases of other family members within a certain age. See Buying Kids on an iPad.

Watch and download music, movies, or TV shows that you or your family have purchased

In the iTunes Store, tap Buy.

If you've set up Family Sharing, click on the items I purchased and then select the family member to view the purchases.

Note: You can only see it if you share your family members' purchases.

Click Music, Movies, or TV.

Find what you want to download, and then click Download.

View your complete iTunes purchase history

Check your iTunes purchase history for purchased apps, songbooks, and more. On your list.

In your purchase history, you can:

• Check when orders are paid into your account.

• See the date of purchase.

• Send e-mail receipts.

• Report a problem with the content you purchased.

• Set content limits

After removing the content and privacy restrictions, go to Settings> Screen Time> Content and Privacy Restrictions> Content Restriction and set the existing restrictions.

CHAPTER TEN

MUSIC

Download music to your iPad

Use the Music app to enjoy your iPad and music over the Internet. With Apple Music Pickers, you can listen to millions of songs without ads and search for music with your friends.

Warning: For important information about preventing hearing loss, see Important iPad Safety Information.

Find music to play on the iPad in the following ways:

Become an Apple Music Subscriber:

You can stream as much music as you want from your Apple Music Directory and music library with a subscription using Wi-Fi or a mobile connection

Note: Services and services are not available in all countries or regions, and articles may vary by region. There is an additional charge for using a mobile connection.

Join Family Sharing: Buy an Apple Family Music membership and everyone in your family sharing group can enjoy Apple Music. You can view your shared subscription and storage on iCloud and family on your iPad.

Purchase music from the iTunes Store: Learn how to search for music, movies,

TV shows, and more on the iPad iTunes Store.

Apple Music Radio: Music Radio broadcasts to Apple Music on three radios worldwide - Apple Music Hits and Apple Music Country. Apple Music Radio is available at music.apple.com on Apple and Android devices, as well as popular web browsers.

View music albums, playlists, and more on iPad

The Music app was purchased from music added and downloaded to Apple Music, music and videos synced to your iPad, TV shows recorded to Apple Music, and the Movie and iTunes Store.

Library screen showing the left sidebar with newly added words. The newly added album is displayed on the right. Player down right.

Look at your music

Under the Library heading, click a category, such as Album or Songs; Click the Download button to view only the music stored on your iPad.

Click on the results and type in the search box to find what you are looking for.

Tap to switch to the album or playlist, click Play or Suffer.

Touch and hold the album art, then click Play.

To change the category list, click Edit in the sidebar, and then select the categories that you want to add, such as the category and collection. Tap any of the available types to remove them.

Your music genre

Under the Library heading, click Playlist, Albums, Songs, TV, and Movies, or Music Videos.

Click Edit, then select a title, artist, newly added, or recently played editing style.

Play shared music on a nearby computer

If a computer on the network shares music at home, you can transfer your music to the iPad.

Choose Settings> Music, click Set Home Sharing, and sign in with your Apple ID.

Open the Music app, click Edit in the sidebar, select Home Sharing, and then click Finish.

Tap Home Sharing, then select Shared Library.

Uninstall the Apple Music app from your iPad

In Settings, tap Music, then turn off the sync directory.

The songs have been deleted from the iPad, but stay in the iCloud app. Purchased or synced music still exists.

Play music on iPad

Use Play In Music now to write lyrics, play, pause, jump, slide, and scroll. You can now use Play to view the pictures in the album and select the next one.

Drive the drive again

You can now use this control Click on the player in the lower right corner to display the Play screen:

Next button.

Skip to the next song. Go fast with the current song.

First button.

Return to the beginning of the song. Click again to play the previous song in the album or playlist. Touch and hold to return to the current song.

Repeat the button.

Click to repeat the disc or playlist. Double-click to repeat a song.

Press the button.

Tap to play songs in sequence. Click again to deactivate the switch.

CHAPTER ELEVEN

APPS

App Store on the iPad

Discover new apps and read stories from the App Store.

Get the app

Ask Siri: You can say Find the app for Arcade games or find the Facebook app

Click one of the following:

Today: Discover specific stories and apps.

Applications: Browse new releases, view top charts, or search for categories.

Search: Type what you want, then click the Search button on your keyboard.

Click on the app to see more information:

• Supported languages

• Compatibility with other Apple devices

• File size

• Screen or preview

• Sports center and family sharing support

• Measurements and reviews

• Confidentiality information

Buy and download the app

To purchase an application, press the Value key.

If you see the download button instead of the value, you have already purchased the app and can download it for free again.

If necessary, verify your Apple ID with a Face ID, Touch ID, or Password to complete your purchase.

The application is downloaded and its icon is displayed on the home screen with a progress bar.

Share or enter the app

Click here for application details.

Click the Share button, then choose Partition, or click the Apple gift (not available in all apps).

Use or send to the Apple Store and iTunes

Click the My Account button or the image in your profile in the upper right corner.

• Use a gift card or code

• E-mail the gift card

Note: You must have an Internet connection and an Apple ID to use the store. Access to the Apple Store and Apple Arcade varies by country and region. The service is available with all featured Apple Arcade content.

Use app clips on iPad

An application clip is a small part of an application that allows you to get the job done quickly without having to download and install the entire application. You will find safaris, maps, messages, or real app clips when you rent a bike, pay for parking, or order food.

Download application clips

To find an app, tap one of the following methods:

Click the clip link in Safari, Maps, or Messages.

Use an iPad camera to scan a QR code that appears in a visible area, such as a restaurant or payment terminal.

The application clip card appears at the bottom of the screen.

You can use Apple Access for supported application clips.

Remove the application clips

Choose Settings> Preview Apps, and then click Remove All App Stores.

Sign up Arcade on your iPad air

You can sign up for Apple Arcade in the App Store to enjoy unlimited access to your collection of games for iPhone, iPad, iPod touch, Mac, and Apple TV.

If you use family sharing, you can share with up to five other family members for free.

Go to the arcade app screen that shows the game and other tips. Click in the upper right corner to manage your profile picture, purchases, and prizes. Below, from left to right, today are sports, programs, arcades, and search tables.

Get the Apple Arcade software

In the App Store, click Arcade, and then do one of the following:

Start with a month of free registration (if you have one): Tap for a free trial.

To start a monthly subscription: Click the Subscribe button.

Check the registration details, then check with your face ID, Touch ID, or Apple ID.

Unsubscribe from Apple Arcade

In the Apple Store, click the My Account button or picture of your profile on the right, then click Sign up.

Tap Apple Arcade, and then click Unsubscribe.

Once you cancel your subscription, you will not be able to play any Apple Arcade if you download it to your device. Delete apps that you no longer need.

You can re-register to play Apple Arcade again and access your game data. Play on iPad

You can find new sports in the Apps and use the Sports Center with your friends.

CHAPTER TWELVE

MAPS

View maps on the iPad

To find your location, you need to connect your iPad to the Internet and unlock Location Services. (See Shared Location on iPad.) For Wi-Fi + mobile models, mobile data charges may apply. (View or change your mobile settings on iPad.)

Warning: For travel and tourism information that can lead to good events, look for important iPad safety information.

Display your current location

Click the Search button.

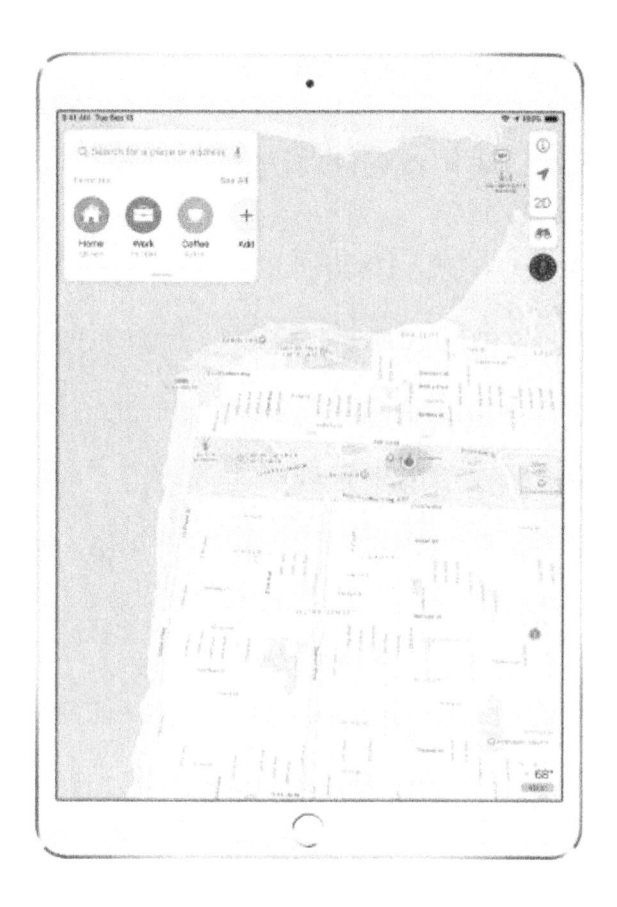

Your location is indicated in the middle of the map. It's at the top of the map. Click the Search button to display it at the top of the title. Click the Search Guide or Compass button to continue viewing above.

Map showing the current location of the city park.

Choose between route, public transit, and satellite view

Click Settings, select Map, Traffic, or Satellite, and then click Close.

If travel information is not available, click View systems for public use or other modes of transportation.

Move, zoom and rotate the map

Rotate the map: Drag the map.

Zoom in or out: Double-click and hold on the screen, then drag up to zoom in or out. Either open or close the map.

The scale appears in the upper left corner as you zoom in. To change the distance, go to Settings> Maps and select miles or kilometers.

Rotate the map: Tap the map with two fingers and rotate your fingers.

After rotating the map to appear at the top of the screen, click the Compass button.

2D model or travel map: swipe two fingers up.

On a 2D satellite map: Click on the 3D on the right.

While viewing the 3D map, you can:

To adjust the angle: Swipe two fingers up or down.

View buildings and other 3D objects: Zoom.

Back to the 2D map: Click on the 2D on the right.

Allow maps to use our location

Maps work best when the right place is open to help you find your location and provide directions to your destination.

To unlock the correct location, follow these steps:

Select Settings> Privacy> Location Services.

Click Maps and open the appropriate location.

You can search for places on the iPad map

Use the Maps app to find addresses, landmarks, services, and more.

Find a place

Ask Siri. You can say: Show me google earth. Learn how to ask Siri.

Or you can click the search button and start typing.

A search card that displays the search term "8th and market" with a number of options.

You can look at it in different ways. For example:

- Intersection ("8th and sales")

- Region ("Greenwich Village")

- Landmark ("Guggenheim")

- Postcode ("60622")

Business ("Movies", "San Francisco CA Restaurants", "Apple Inc. New York")

Drag the search tab to see all the results. Tap to view the result guide.

Note: If you see an information card instead of a search section, click Close in the upper-right corner of the information card.

You can quickly find or delete recently searched items

To see a list of recently viewed search results swipe from the bottom of the search tab.

To delete an item from the list, slide your finger on the remaining item. Or click to see everything directly in the list, then do one of the following:

Delete a group: Click on the top of the group.

To delete an item: Slide the remaining item with your finger.

Delete key features of the iPad.

Find nearby landmarks and services on iPad Maps

Use Maps to find nearby places, services, and more.

Find a service nearby

Ask Siri. You can tell me to look for a grocery store or find a cafe near me. Learn how to ask Siri.

Or click on the search bar and click on a category like a restaurant or a hotel and do the following:

To see all the results in the list: Slide your finger on the info card.

To change the search location: Drag or zoom the map to another location, then click the Search button at the top of the screen.

To see more results: Click an item on the info card.

About four types of services appear on the search tab on the left side of the screen. These include restaurants, catering, food delivery, and gas stations.

CHAPTER THIRTEEN

KEYBOARD

Apple external keyboard for iPad

These full-size (sold separately) mobile devices allow you to insert text while watching the iPad in full.

Magic keyboard for iPad

The iPad's magic keyboard connects directly to the iPad and closes, forming a small-cap (support formats). It includes a built-in trackpad that lets you browse the iPad screen, open apps, and more. IPad's magic keyboard doesn't need a battery or external power (but you can combine it with power to keep the iPad charged).

Appropriate keyboard

The smart keyboard connects directly to the iPad and becomes a thin cover. The keyboard does not require batteries or an external power source.

Connect the appropriate keyboard to the iPad.

Magical keyboard

The Magic Keyboard integrates with the iPad via Bluetooth, including the Microsoft Keyboard Number keyboard. The Magic Keyboard is powered by a rechargeable battery.

Insert a magic keyboard for iPad (with the built-in trackpad)

To connect and use the Bluetooth version of Magic Keyboard, see the dual Magic Keyboard on the iPad.

Connect the magic keyboard to the iPad

Open the keyboard, bend it again, and glue the iPad.

Microsoft has opened and folded the iPad keyboard. Magic for iPad is located on the Magic Keyboard clipboard.

To adjust the angle of view, press the iPad as needed.

Note: If you turn off the keyboard to cover the 12.9-inch (4th generation) or

11-inch (2nd generation) iPad Pro during video or audio, the phone is always active, but the iPad's microphone is muted. If you use AirPods or other headphones, you can continue the conversation.

Adjust the brightness of the keyboard

Go to Settings> General> Keyboard> Computer Hardware and drag the slider to change the brightness level in low light conditions.

Charge your iPad while using the Microsoft iPad keyboard

Connect the keyboard to a power source with the USB-C charging cable and USB-C AC adapter that came with the iPad.

Important: The Magic Magic Keyboard for iPad includes a magnet that holds the iPad securely. Be careful not to store information stored on electronic magnets, such as credit cards or important hotel cards, on the Magic Keyboard or between the iPad and Microsoft Keyboard.

Switch to an on-screen keyboard or other language keyboard on iPad

If you want to do this, use the on-screen keyboard instead of the external keyboard.

Switch to the on-screen keyboard

Press the keyboard shortcut (at the bottom of the screen) on the command bar, and then press the keyboard key.

To hide the on-screen keyboard, press the Hide Keyboard button.

Switch between language keyboards

To switch between English and other keyboard layouts, press and hold the scroll key, and then press the space bar.

Tip: To add other languages, press the Caps Lock key to switch between Latin and the other keyboard you are using.

To change the language, disable the Caps Lock switch, go to Settings> General> Keyboard> Hardware Keyboard, and then clear the case change.

Capture the text while using Apple's external keyboard on iPad

You can order text instead of typing on the iPad.

Make sure the icon is enabled in Settings> General> Keyboard.

Note: This setting may not be available in all languages or all countries or regions, and scores may vary. They can be mobile data payments. You can view or change your mobile settings on the iPad.

CHAPTER FOURTEEN

REMINDER

Set reminders for iPad

With Reminder, you can easily create and organize reminders so you can easily learn what to do. Use it for shopping lists, work projects, homework, and anything else you want to keep an eye on. Perform subtasks, set markers, add attachments, and when and when to receive reminders. You can use a good list to automatically prepare reminders.

A reminder screen that lists the monuments on the left and the visitor camps on the right. When done, click on the reminder.

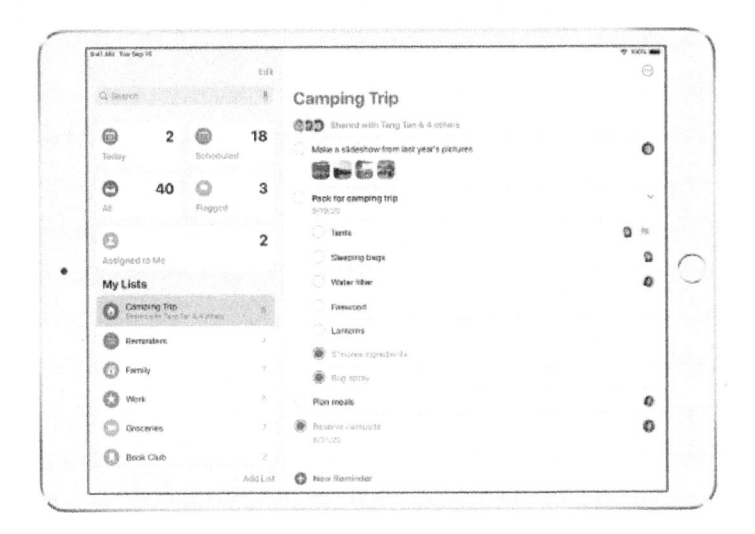

iCloud reminders — and any changes you make to them — appear on your iPhone, iPad, iPod touch, Apple Watch, and Mac when you sign in with your iPhone ID.

Note: If you're using iOS 12 or earlier, you may want to update your iCloud reminders to use attachments, flags, folders, group lists, color lists, icons, and more. (Click the top left corner to view your iCloud account.)

Updated reminders don't lag behind reminders from previous versions of iOS and macOS. See iOS 13 app analysis.

Add a reminder

Ask Siri. Say something like, "Add Articox to the menu

Or do the following:

Tap New reminder, then enter the text. Or if you have an Apple pencil, write to the next section.

Use the quick toolbar at the top of the table to do the following:

Date & Schedule: Press the Date & Time button, then select when you want to be reminded.

Add a place: Click the place button, then select the place you want to remind.

Note: To get location-based reminders, you must allow reminders to use your location. Go to Settings> Privacy> Local Services, create location services, click Reminders, select while using the app, and create the appropriate location.

Add a reminder: (Available in the shared list) Click the People button, then select someone (including you) from the shared list.

Set an indicator: Press the indicator button to mark an important reminder.

Attach a photo or scanned document: Click the Photo button, then take a new photo, select an existing photo in the photo library, or scan a document.

To add more information to the reminder, press Edit Details, and then do the following:

Add notes: In the Notes box, type more information about the reminder.

Add a web link: You can enter a web address in the URL field. Reminders show the link as a thumbnail that you can click on the site.

You will be reminded when you chat with someone in messages: Create "Send Messages" and select someone from your contacts list. Reminders will arrive the next time you talk to that person about text messages.

Forward setting: Click on the first location and then select an option.

Tip: After OS X 10.10 or later, you can transfer fixed reminders between Mac and iPad.

Mark the reminder in its entirety

Press the blank circle next to the reminder, mark it perfectly, and hide it.

To hide completed reminders, press further, and finish the display.

Organize multiple reminders at once

Press Next, select Reminders and then select the reminders you want to edit. Or swipe two fingers for the reminders you want to edit.

Use the buttons at the bottom of the screen to fill in, mark, add, move, delete, or delete selected reminders.

Move or delete reminders

To arrange reminders in a list: Tap the reminder you want to zoom in and drag it to a new location.

To perform a low task: Slide the reminder to the right, and then click

Indent. Or drag the reminder to another reminder.

If you delete or move the parent functions, the following functions will also be deleted. If you fulfill the parent role, the lower tasks are fulfilled.

To move a reminder to another list: Press Reminder, click Edit, click List, and select List.

Delete a reminder: Swipe left on the reminder, and then click Delete.

Tip: To delete a reminder with an Apple stylus, overwrite the reminder.

To retrieve a deleted reminder, slide your finger or slide your finger to delete it

CHAPTER FIFTEEN

HOME APP

Set up accessories using iPad Home

When you first activate the Home application, the Setup Assistant helps you create a home where you can add devices and define rooms. If you have already created a home using another custom home kit application, skip this step.

Add the device to your home

Before you add a device, such as a lamp or a camera, make sure it's plugged in, activated, and using a Wi-Fi network.

In the sidebar, tap Home, and then click Add.

Tap Add Device, then follow the onscreen instructions.

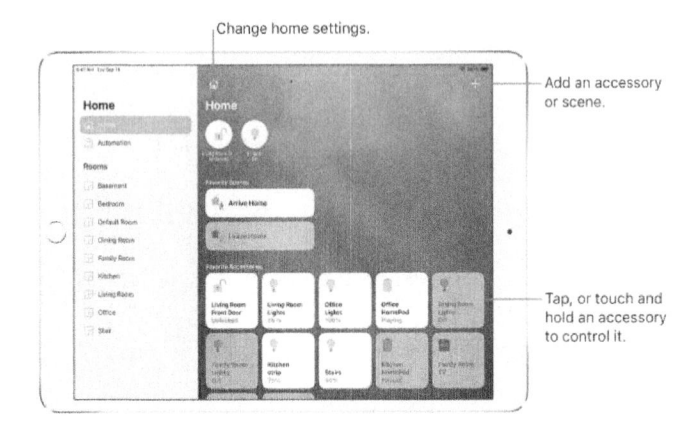

When adding a device, assign a room or a room of your choice.

You need to scan the QR code or enter the 8-digit original stock code (or its box or document) into the device itself. A well-supported TV shows the QR code for scanning. You can assign a device to a room and give it a name, and then use that name when managing the device with Siri. You can add the recommended automation during installation.

When you set up an Apple TV in tvOS and share it in a room, it automatically appears in the room's Home app.

Change the entrance room quota

• In the sidebar, select the currently selected room.

• If not already assigned, search for the default room.

• Press and hold the tool key, and then press and hold or press the Settings key.

• Tap a room, then select a room.

• Open Add to Favorites to grant Home access.

To rearrange your favorites, click Add and Edit Home Page, click Edit Screen, and drag the access settings to the setting you want. Tap when you tap when done.

Housing system with left side strip. The living room is shown in the sidebar. On the right are the status buttons for the top two headlights, the two areas at the bottom, and the three input buttons at the bottom.

Arrange rooms in the areas

Join Siri in a convenient location to control different areas of your home. For example, if you have a two-story house, you can book rooms in the basement of the first floor. you can tell him to turn off the lights for Siri.

Click Add and Edit Home Page, and then click Settings.

Tap Zone, click an existing location or click Create New to add a room to a new location.

Decorate the room

You can change the room name and wallpaper, add a room to the name, or empty the room. When you leave a room, the dedicated resources are transferred to the normal room.

Click Add and Edit Home Page, and then click Room Settings.

Click on a room and make your own changes.

Manage devices and home on iPad

Manage your home application tools

Tap Home or Next Room, then press and hold the enter button to quickly turn the device on or off - press and hold until the light or control appears.

Existing controls depend on the type of access. For example, some bulbs have a color change. You can use Smart TV to select the installation source.

Management Center Management Tools

When you're at home with your iPad and you open the Control Center, you'll see the right scenes and devices at this moment. For example, a coffee maker will appear in the morning to replace the night light at night.

Press or hold the button to open the device, or press and hold the button until the controller appears. Open the Control Center to quickly view your favorite furniture, then click the Home button.

If you do not want to see Devices in the Control Center, go to Settings> Control Center and disable the Manage Home Management feature.

Set up household appliances

To edit device settings, touch and hold the device button, press or hold the Settings button, and then do the following:

To rename an item: Click Delete to delete the old word, then type the new one.

To change a device icon: Click the icon next to the device name, then select New Icon. If you do not find an option in some icons, it means that the icon cannot be changed from the existing one.

Team tools

You can have a lot of control by working with the button pump.

Tap and hold a device, slide it across the screen, or press Options, and then click Groups and more.

Press the device you want to connect to this object - for example, another lamp in the room.

enter the group name in the group.

If you'd like To display the group on the Home tab, enter Open Favorites.

Check the condition of your home

The housing system indicates the problems that need to be addressed

Printed in Great Britain
by Amazon